The Life and Times of Dan Haggerty

...the man who made Grizzly Adams Famous!

"*The Preacher, the Pirate and the Pagan*"

by: TERRY W. BOMAR

Copyright © 2013 Terry W. Bomar

All rights reserved.

ISBN-10:1492189928
ISBN-13: 9781492189923

DEDICATION

This book is lovingly dedicated in memory of

Samantha Haggerty

June E. Bomar

and "Wild Bill" William Stallings

CONTENTS

	Acknowledgments	I
1	In The Booth	3
2	The Preacher, Death and Dinner	11
3	Beware of Preachers Wearing T-Shirts	21
4	The Three Opposites	31
5	Away We Go	41
6	A New Tour Begins	55
7	Trumped	65
8	Wild Bill	73
9	Castles, Boats & Bears	81
10	A Real World Education	91
11	The Inside Passage	99
12	Now There are Two	109

ACKNOWLEDGMENTS

I would like to thank all the friends and fans of Dan Haggerty, that love him and the peaceful world that his portrayal of Grizzly Adams represented.

The Preacher, the Pirate, and the Pagan
is just the first of many volumes to come in this:

Life and Times of Dan Haggerty Book Series

In this book series you will discover the amazing tales of Dan Haggerty's life; before he was famous, how it all started, and his personal experiences with the super stars of yesterday.
You will be shocked by the unbelievable stories of tragedies and triumphs that went on behind the scenes of the show about the life of James Capen "Grizzly" Adams.

"The true stories that no one has ever dared to tell before!

In the Booth

I am always amazed when I take my seat in the booth.

The table in front of me is filled with 8x10 glossy photos, water bottles, personalized coffee cups and video tape sets from a TV show that aired 35 years ago. The people are lined up; some are holding action figures, posters, lunch boxes, trash cans, board games and a dozen other collectibles. The people all have the same goal; they want to meet the man sitting beside me. Behind his famous beard is a big smile and an infectious laugh that captures the room. His stories make everyone laugh and his sincere love for his fans make each one of them feel special.

I have to smile as I watch an endless parade on men, women and children step up to get an autographed picture; or to have him sign their *"Grizzly Adams Action Figure"* or some other collectable that someone has held on to since the 70's. The ladies all want to get a *"bear hug"* and a picture with the man they idolized in the *"good ole days"* of television.

Every chance I get when the line dies down I ask him a question (usually with a smirk on my face), *"what in world was so special about that crazy show that makes this many people love you so much?"* He usually answers with some quick witted remark, *"it must have been the bear."*

He is the *"big celebrity"* (as I tease him), and I'm just there to add variety. It's crazy, we're almost exact opposites and yet the best of friends for nearly two decades. We bicker, banter, laugh and cut up all day long. I make fun

of the show and he makes fun of me ...and that's the way it goes hour after hour, day after day a dozen weekends a year.

It's a good question don't you think, *"What is it about that ole show that was so special and why is the name Grizzly Adams such an icon?"*

We have traveled in Europe and all across America in every state including Alaska and Hawaii; and we even get mail from as far away as Australia and Japan hearing from fans that love the show and Dan Haggerty. I am biased, but what I've seen and heard tells me that people really do want more family television. They're yearning for the simpler times with real family values; and basic respect for each other and for the world we live in. I think those people are right. We desperately need more television that focuses on the better nature of mankind instead of the constant flood of *"easy money"* programing that highlights the very worst in human behavior.

There was something magical about that gentle man *"James Adams,"* walking around with his big ole bear named *"Ben"*. His Native American *"blood brother, Nakoma"* and *"Mad Jack"* with his stubborn ole mule *"Number 7"* added to the family fun. Even the production of the show lacked sophistication; but the simplicity and sincerity of the characters and the message of simple values came through the screen and captured a generation of people. It still stirs them 35 years later.

When you say the name *Grizzly Adams,* it brings up mental images of beautiful wilderness, a giant grizzly bear lumbering through the forest and a soft spoken mountain man with a huge beard. It certainly doesn't bring up the true story of the real Grizzly Adams that lived in the 1800's. Most people don't even know that there was a *"real" Grizzly Adams,* known as James Capen *"Grizzly"* Adams. Most people don't even think about the novel that Chuck Sellier wrote that *"sanitized"* the real Grizzly Adams into a mountain man that never killed anything (opposite from the real character), which gave birth to the film and television series.

The Life and Times of Dan Haggerty

When you say *Grizzly Adams*, most people think of the beard first, and then the gentle man that wore it. It was Dan Haggerty and the character he played that made Grizzly Adams a household name. A few years ago I saw a report that said that the third most recognizable name in America in the late 70's was Dan Haggerty ...just ahead of President Jimmy Carter.

The future editions of this *Life and Times of Dan Haggerty Book Series,* will go into great detail about the crazy stories on the set and behind the scenes of the show that will shock you. They'll cover the ridiculous stories and bazaar battles that surround the man, the name, the film and television show that people know as *Grizzly Adams.* If you like drama, you don't want to miss this! In the almost two decades that I have been involved; I have never seen anything like it!

Now that I have teased you with the true stories to come, I will say this; it drives *certain people* crazy that all of America knows that it was Dan Haggerty that made Grizzly Adams famous. Without his big smile and gentle manner behind the unique beard that Dan brought to the character, there would be no brand and few would even remember the show.

Believe it or not, I never watched the old show (which is a great source of humor between us). But now after over 15 years of friendship and business, as I watch the newly released videos I am amazed at how much of the *James Adams* character ...is really Dan Haggerty! The exact phrases, mannerisms, movements and even some of the thought processes are purely Dan Haggerty. I broke out into laughter because they certainly weren't scripted. Then of course, I made a call to Dan to make fun and point out all the mistakes! (By now, you should be starting to get an idea of the kind of friendship we really have.)

During many management conversations I am often asked, *"what kind of celebrity is Dan Haggerty?"* My answer has always been the same: *"he is by far the best celebrity I've ever dealt with because he always gives the client more time than they asked for and fills the room with excitement, fun and laughter, wherever he goes."* As I watch him deal with his fans, I can see the same patience and gentleness that made his character famous. However, unlike his famous character, Dan definitely has a *wild side* that's NOT associated with the woods!

It makes my hands hurt when I think about all those people lining up for an autograph; but Dan loves spending time with fans and you can see it with every autograph he signs.

He doesn't just scribble his initials like most celebs do; he addresses each one personally with a note and then adds his unique signature along with the date and paw print from *"Ben"*. If the paw isn't there ...Dan didn't sign it!

One thing that is truly amazing for me is the patience Dan has while he answers the same questions over and over and over again. I admire the fact that even though he's already answered the same question fifty times that day, he makes each person feel like they were the first one to ask it.

It's actually quite a lot of fun to travel to nice locations and sit "in the booth." We meet other celebrities and share our "war stories." We meet old and new fans and fill the days with laughter ...you can't beat it.

We're always working on the last film project or planning the next one. We're acting, producing, or writing scripts and searching for sponsors. The development work never stops, so the personal appearances and autograph signings are great way to stay in touch with fans and old friends.

It's refreshing and always interesting especially when you have a few funny fans thrown in; like the those that believe he is just a guy "faking it" ….and that's no joke.

Of course it's always fun for me when I hear somebody walk up to the booth, look Dan in the eye and say so sincerely: "I thought you were dead!"

And there I go …rolling in the floor laughing again.

The Preacher...
Death and Dinner

I had no idea how my life was about to change as I left the Los Angeles Airport.

I stopped to tour the Hollywood Bowl before I headed to Studio City. I drove past the famous *Hollywood Sign* that looks down upon the city that has made so many celebrities famous; and I was about to meet with one of them.

I settled into my room at *The Sportsman's Lodge*, which is another famed landmark that *once upon a time* was frequented by such Hollywood greats as John Wayne, Lauren Bacall, Lena Horne and many more. I was there for a few days of meetings with actor *Doug McClure,* who is best remembered for his long running role as *Trampas* in the popular western television series *The Virginian*.

It was the early 90's and this was all new to me because at that time I had already been a licensed minister for sixteen years. My life up to this point had been totally focused on ministry. I had spent years pastoring three churches, doing missionary work and serving as a prison chaplain.

I never dreamed that I would be involved with Hollywood in any fashion; but here I was waiting for *Doug McClure* to arrive for our first scheduled breakfast meeting. While still pastoring a church in 1992, I founded a nonprofit mentoring organization called Young Adventurers and we were in search of National Celebrity Spokesperson. A key part of our organization is focused on adventure and stretching your limits, so we needed someone special who was rugged, wild and ready for a challenge.

We had already taken kids across America touring museums, historic landmarks and National Parks. We went white water rafting, mountain climbing, riding horses and helicopters. So when the tall rugged McClure stood up and insisted that he wanted ride *"with the kids"* when we made our next cross country trip, I knew that Doug was our man!

We worked out the details and both of us were genuinely excited about the future. I was amazed at how welcoming and enthusiastic this "star" was about helping kids. He was truly a wonderful guy and we began immediately planning our next trip.

Since Doug was a star from the old western television shows, we planned the *"Wild West Stampede."* We would take selected kids from all backgrounds on a cross country adventure.

We traveled from South Florida through the Civil War battlefields, across the prairies, went camping at the Grand Canyon; and traveled on to the "back lots" of Hollywood. Our kids would join *Craig T. Nelson, Jerry Van Dyke* and *Shelly Fabares* for a "live" taping of the "Coach" TV show. After the taping we joined the cast and crew for and dinner on the set.

For the trip home, we took the *southern route* and hiked the Guadalupe Mountains and explored the Carlsbad Caverns. In Texas we stopped at site of President John F. Kennedy's assassination; and toured the museum on the sixth floor of the Texas School Book Depository where Lee Harvey Oswald fired the fatal shots. We crossed the mighty Mississippi into New Orleans and traveled on to Disney World and finally back home to South Florida.

The "Wild West Stampede" was a major success! It changed the lives of every kid and volunteer that was involved. One boy had just lost his father to suicide, a few kids were from *the hood* and three were students from a high school TV production class. The kids filmed the entire trip interviewing stars and recording all the adventure.

We made the trip and Doug was *with us* ...but he wasn't *"riding with the kids"* as he so desperately wanted to do.

> "Doug was one of the kindest men
>
> I've ever known."

Doug's finger prints and inspiration was with us every mile along the way, but Doug was back in Sherman Oaks, California fighting for his life. He had recently been diagnosed with lung cancer. His health made it impossible for him to take his first adventure with the kids that he had been anxiously looking forward to lead.

For Doug the next several months were consumed with waging the battle against cancer.

On December 16th 1994, he appeared in public to receive his "star" on the famed Hollywood Blvd.

He was still acting at the time but on January 8th he collapsed from an apparent stroke on the film set of *"One West Waikiki"* in Hawaii. He was flown back to California where the Doctors discovered that the cancer had spread from his lungs, to his liver and bones. On February 5th 1995, Doug McClure died. He was buried in Woodlawn Memorial Cemetery in Santa Monica, California.

I have to agree with one of Doug's friends who said:
"Doug was one of the kindest men
I've ever known."

We stayed in touch during the course of his illness and we spoke often. Every time he asked about the Young Adventurers and how the kids were doing.

My last conversation with Doug was shortly before his death and it was wonderful. He was so happy for me and the success of the trip and sent all the kids his love. Then we prayed together for several minutes. He was in a great mood and assured me that he was in total peace and that he had complete trust and faith in Jesus Christ.

Wow, what a phone call!

We never spoke again, but we will one day
...one day real soon!

It took a while to regroup, but before long I was back out in Hollywood looking for a spokesman. Once again I was sitting by the pool at *The Sportsman's Lodge* where Doug and I had first met; but things weren't going so well this time. Every meeting so far had turned up nothing but mismatches and I wasn't looking forward to making that long flight back home empty handed.

Then my phone rang. It wasn't quite like *"the shot heard around the world,"* but sometimes it feels that way! The voice of my friend on the other end of the line said: *"have you thought about Grizzly Adams?"* I replied, *"Not lately, I never watched the show, why?"* My friend was shocked, *"are you kidding me? He would be perfect for you and the Young Adventurers!"* After a few minutes he made the call to set up a meeting. The next day a big man with a beard walked into *The Sportsman's Lodge!*

I met him in the lobby; he was right on time and with a big smile and firm handshake he said:
"Hi, I'm Dan Haggerty."

The connection was immediate, just like it had been with Doug McClure. In less than an hour we had moved on from business to laughter; and that's when I made my first mistake.

"Mr. Haggerty, I would love to take you dinner tonight – and you can pick the place!" Haggerty didn't bat an eye, "How about the Bistro Gardens, right here in Studio City?"

> **Note:** Any time a young southern preacher goes to Los Angeles and invites a celebrity to dinner and allows them to *"pick the place"* in Hollywood ... is a mistake!

I said: *"That sounds great to me..."*
and with those five simple words I was hooked.

A few hours later, as a party of four we all enjoyed an unbelievable dinner. It was a wonderful evening filled with lots of laughter and a lot of plans. When the night was over we all friends and happy about the possibilities.

However, I've never let him forget that he was an expensive "first date" when they handed me the $800 bill!

As I paid the check I couldn't help but think

>...maybe I should not have answered
>my phone when it rang...

Beware of Preachers Wearing T-Shirts

We had become instant friends but in business, to say that Dan and I got off to a slow start is an understatement. He was in Los Angeles, California and I lived in Palm Beach County, Florida. It wasn't just the 2,700 miles that separated us; he lived in a very different world.

My entire life has been centered around the ministry and nonprofit work - and it still is. His entire life has revolved around film, television, acting and Hollywood – and he still is. For him it was business but this was also an opportunity that many celebrities enjoy. It was a chance to give back, help some kids and have some fun in the process. For me it was business too; I wanted his rugged celebrity to spark some interest in my charity, inspire some kids and hopefully have some fun in the process as well. I can absolutely tell you that the "fun part" has been incredible; but in the words of *Seinfeld's* George Costanza, what neither of us expected was what would happen when *"Worlds Collide!"*

Maybe it was coincidence, karma or just preparation for a new direction; but change was blowing in the wind. First, a hurricane swept through and damaged my home in South Florida. Then it wasn't long before a tornado ripped across my property in Tennessee blowing the log home I was building right off the foundation. My charity, after a decade of receiving grants from the state of Florida to run Young Adventurers in a dozen south Florida schools, the Juvenile Justice Department funding was several cut back and we were left empty handed.

In mere moments Young Adventurers had lost its annual grant and primary source of funding. To make matters worse, the Sheriff that we had worked with for so long died suddenly, also from lung cancer just like Doug McClure. Because of the death of the Sheriff and a new administration coming in during hard financial times we lost our secondary funding from the local Sheriff's Department as well. I finally had our "National Celebrity Spokesman" but now we had no more money.

We had worked with a dozen schools with in-house and after-school programs every day for ten years and served over 12,000 kids and families. We had travelled over a 100 thousand miles running adventure trips and projects all across America. There was no way I was going to quit now; I just needed a new plan.

I must admit that the unexpected "disasters" were everywhere. But since those days Dan and I both have come to realize that all the things that failed have been balanced by too many incredible events and opportunities to count. In the middle of all the confusion I didn't realize that some new adventures were about to begin; and it all started with a T-Shirt.

The charity needed money immediately and all our *"big sources"* were gone. So I decided to conduct some easy, small fund raisers to create awareness and generate cash. When I saw a summer sports show sign hanging over the *Bass Pro Shop* it gave me an idea. The question was, could I get Dan to buy it? I pitched *Bass Pro Shop* for an appearance with *Dan Haggerty*, the man that made *Grizzly Adams* famous. They loved it; and it wasn't long before I had Dan on a plane to Florida to represent Young Adventurers for the first time. It would be a three day Outdoor Sports Show and the first time we would work together.

This would be a week surprises for Mr. Haggerty and it started at the airport. It's customary to have a representative meet the celebrity at the airport with a limo waiting curbside to provide transportation to the hotel or event. But not me, I wanted to make this personal; after all I was a "southern" preacher and I wanted to share some of our famous *"southern hospitality."*

I decided that I would pick him up personally in my new Jaguar that I had just gotten a few months before. What I didn't think about was the gridlock that awaited me on I-95, a few miles away. When Mr. Haggerty's plane touched down I was sitting in Florida's newly formed *"parking lot"* on what was once a busy Interstate just an hour ago. Thirty minutes later when I finally pulled up to the airport all the passengers where gone! I had never seen it so dead, even the baggage handlers were just sitting around. I was totally embarrassed and panicked. Surely I was the first idiot in history to "lose a celebrity" on the very first event!

I made one more circle through baggage claim and spotted him. He was just sitting in the same place he had been sitting all along - enjoying some of our fabulous South Florida humidity. It was so sweltering hot I was surprised that his beard hadn't curled. I was even more surprised that he wasn't mad at all. He was full of sarcastic humor though; and he wasn't about to let me forget what just happened!

We are total opposites in many ways but we were like brothers from the start. The laughter began as soon as he got in the car and I soon learned a fascinating fact about Dan. He has an amazing eye for details. It started as a joke when he pointed out all the patterns in the wood grained dashboard that looked like the faces and forms of Grizzly Bears. I laughed at first but quickly realized that he appreciated the smallest details in everything; flowers, trees, cars, animals, birds – you name it! It was the first thing I learned about Dan Haggerty. I learned that behind the beard and big smile, beyond the celebrity image, he has a genuine appreciation for life – it all its forms. .

He had no idea what my plan was when he turned and asked me which Hotel he was booked in; he thought that he was making another ordinary appearance for autograph signings. I had no idea that he seldom ever would stay in a private home. So much for my "southern hospitality" and it was about to get much, much worse! I finally broke the news to him that the plan was for him to make the appearance but the object was to find new sponsors and contributions for Young Adventurers; oh yeah ...and sell T-Shirts! After all ...what are brothers for?

He knew that he had been *"snookered"* by the *"ah shucks style"* of this Tennessee Preacher; but from the smirk on his face, I knew he kinda liked it. So I figured it was a good time to let him know that we weren't going to the Hilton, we were going to my house. We had just bought a beautiful home on the lake surrounded by palm trees and I assured him that he would love it when he saw the place. What I didn't know was that in a few hours my tropical

home sweet home would turn into *"Home SWEAT Home!"*

By the time we turned into the lakefront community he had relaxed and was once again pointing out unique plants and trees that I hadn't seen before in the year that I had lived there. Next he spotted a red-tail hawk; like he does almost every time I ride with him. It's amazing - through the years regardless of where we are – he notices the most exotic birds! The guy loves birds, especially birds of prey like Eagles and Hawks. Through the years he has rescued, caught and trained many hawks. At an early age he began teaching his son Cody about falconry. Today as young man Cody shares his father's love for birds and is licensed with several agencies that care for birds of prey.

I was right; when he walked into my home he loved it! The patio and pool looked out over the peaceful lake where ducks greeted us every evening and a pesky pelican would often make his appearance in the morning. But it wouldn't be long before this peaceful serenity would shatter into chaos.

I noticed that it was a little warm in the house as we began making plans for the next day's event at Bass Pro Shop. On the ride home Dan had fully accepted the idea of selling T-Shirts (he had no choice), but true to form and his attention to detail he wanted to make them better. He searched through his bag until he found a drawing that he had done years ago and handed it to me.

The second thing I learned about Dan Haggerty that day was that he is an amazing artist. His drawings were incredible. He excels at anything artistic. When he was younger he spent years sculpting, craving wood and crafting leather. When he handed me the drawing he said *"this could represent the wild and courageous spirit of Young Adventurers; do you think you could add it to your T-shirts?"*

I loved the drawing and raced it over to my T-shirt maker. By the next day he had a box of T-shirts waiting for us when we arrived at the booth. When I got back home late that evening Dan was already asleep. I noticed it was a lot warmer in the house but I didn't think too much about it. I turned the AC down and went to bed because tomorrow was going to be a long day.

> It was 2 a.m. when I was awaken
> by a scream in the night!

It wasn't a fearful scream but it sounded like a disaster was coming from Dan's room. Half asleep I ran across the house and down the hall. I don't know why …but when I saw Grizzly Adams standing there in the middle of a bedroom filled with 3 inches of water I exploded in hysterical laughter! It took a minute for Dan to join in …but soon both of us had tears running down our faces laughing as we desperately tried to stop the flood or start building an Ark!

Dan wasn't about to tread water waiting for an AC guy to come out; so we broke out the tools determined to fix it ourselves. It took a while to get to it, but we finally found the pipe that had broken deep in the system. I wonder what the neighbors thought when they saw a big bearded guy working outside our house at three o'clock in the morning?

We ran new pipe, repaired the unit and cleaned up the swimming pool that was in Dan's room. By then it was almost daylight, but finally it was fixed. With a grin and a grunt, like an ole grizzly bear Dan just lumbered back to his cave and went back to sleep.

In a few hours we were both in the booth selling T-shirts and autographs. It took some extra coffee but no one knew the saga that was behind the beard that day. Bass Pro Shop was thrilled; and the people turned out in droves. Everyone loved Dan and we sold a lot of T-shirts!

Young Adventurers made some good money and a lot of new friends. It had been a great day and lot of fun. Now, we were looking forward to getting home to a cool house and nice dinner.

We needed some rest to be ready for tomorrow and I couldn't wait to get in the car to go home. I loved that car - it was my quiet place to enjoy music and relax. I already had it running when Dan opened the door and dropped exhaustedly into the passenger seat. That's when I heard a strange *"tearing"* sound ...and my heart sunk for a moment.

Well... at least I can always brag that the comb in the back pocket of Grizzly Adams put a four inch rip in my new Jag's leather seat.

Instead, I just added it to stack of other crazy things we laugh about...

Life is too short to stress the small stuff!

The Life and Times of Dan Haggerty

The Three Opposites

If it's not broke ...don't fix it! Repeat it!

It wasn't long after Dan returned to L.A. that I figured if it worked once – it'll work again.

So I took the same formula and set up our next event. The next time it was the *Ducks Unlimited Ultimate Sports Show* in my hometown of Memphis, Tennessee. After that we went back to South Florida; then to South Carolina, Detroit, Michigan and finally to Orlando where we would connect a deal that would launch a whole new road trip.

> It was official ...this was the summer of
> *T-Shirts on Tour!*

Terry W. Bomar

So far, my entire friendship with Dan had consisted of an introduction, one expensive dinner, three days in a booth and one night splashing around in our in-home water park at 3 a.m. Now we were about to meet once each month for three or four days of craziness. It would be on these trips that he would get to know the *preacher* and I would meet the *pirate and the pagan.*

It was in the Marriott Hotel in Memphis when I first met William "Wild Bill" Stallings; aka *the Pagan.* I didn't know it at the time but he would be one of most interesting men and closest friends I would ever know. He was strolling across the lobby when Dan walked up to me and said, *"I want you to meet my brother Bill."*

> **Note:** Even though we three would work closely together on numerous projects in the future, it would be <u>a year</u> before I learned that Bill wasn't his brother – he was only *"like a brother."*

Surprised I said, *"Wow, I didn't know you had a brother!"* Dan does have brothers but Bill wasn't one of them. Those are the type of *"details"* Dan doesn't pay much attention too.

Dan loves to keep you *"off balance"* and keep you guessing; no matter who you are. It must be a source of personal entertainment because I see him do it to others all the time. I just grin and chuckle under my breath. I guess it's the *Pirate* in him... After all these years of friendship I have to laugh because *I still don't know* exactly who's who in all the Haggerty clan. Today I know I am one of Dan's closet friends and I'm not sure if *anyone really knows* this loveable Pirate that millions of fans call Grizzly Adams.

The Memphis show was fairly standard stuff. We were signing autographs, taking pictures and selling more T-Shirts; with a few exceptions. We did have a couple of wild and crazy surprises. On the wild side ...our friend and actor, *Jeff Watson* showed up with *Brody*, his 1500 lb. grizzly bear. My brother stopped

by and provided some craziness. Keith, who is a children's pastor and professional clown invaded our booth dressed as *Tiko the Hobo*.

Dan has never forgotten that big red nose!

It would be the people and personal conversations we had that made Memphis so significant. Dan met most of my family and realized that all of us were very sincere about our faith. It's the guiding force in our lives.

I learned a lot more about Dan too. He was born and raised in Hollywood. We talked about his incredible dad, about the rough times growing up and how he got started in films. Dan was fortunate enough to be friends with many of the classic stars from the *"golden age"* of Hollywood. Robert Mitchum, was like a father to him. Mitchum, nicknamed *(The Goose)* was his mentor and close friend, along with others. Dan was roasted on the *Dean Martin Celebrity Roast* and was close with

Dean and many of the other *"great"* actors of the day.

When the conversation turned toward religion (which it often did with me around) it was always interesting and conflicted. It still is. We come from totally different backgrounds so when we it comes to *"conversations"*...we've had some *"doosies!"*

Dan has always had a sincere respect and admiration for my faith and religion in general; but he has plenty of questions and challenges too. Let me put it this way; he never has been a choir boy and I don't see him *"signing up"* anytime soon. But I have seen the other side too; I remember one night in Memphis when we had a sincere talk and I told him that I really felt that God had put me in his life. I felt it then and still do today ...that is the *"real"* reason we connected. That same night he shared with me some of his personal thoughts and battles and asked me to pray for him and his family – so we did, right then and there.

"Wild Bill" was another story entirely. He never debated, questioned or challenged me. It was almost funny, when a conversation started up he just listened to me until I was finished; then he would shoot it all down saying that he loved and respected me but he was an agnostic and simply didn't believe in anything. And with a smile ...the conversation was over. That's how he got the nickname *"Pagan"* – he picked it out!

It may be hard for you to believe, but as I said before …he would be one of the most interesting men and closest friends I would ever know. He was a walking contradiction. In mannerisms he was quiet and polite but he was also called "Wild Bill" for a reason. He was as wild as they come! The Bill I knew was always kind, generous and very easy going; but he had been married seven times (at least...), served several years in prison; and for while he was a loan shark and an enforcer for a well-known motorcycle gang in California.

It was hard for me to believe all those things about Bill (any many more). He was extremely punctual and honest - especially about money. If he said that he would do something – he did it - and always on time! He expected you to be the same way too. If there was any question about a situation …he would always go the extra mile. If he didn't like you, he wouldn't pretend too. If he did like you, he would show you that he really cared about your well-being. We disagreed on so many things concerning choices and behavior; but just like it was with Dan, we had an instant personal friendship.

In those first few days we formed a strange bond between the three of us. We were polar opposites but we were already very close. We were three complex guys with strong and stubborn personalities. None of us were about to change our positions, but our differences actually became a source of strength for the friendship. Our friendship and *"conversations"* were so odd and funny that the nickname was born: *the Preacher, the Pirate and the Pagan*.

There was unspoken respect and understanding for each other's lives. We always freely expressed our own opinions but we didn't try to change each other. We were just good friends and we kept it that way. The cross I wear around my neck today is one of my most prized possessions because Bill and Dan picked it out together as a gift for me in New Orleans way back in 2005.

In Memphis, they learned about me; that there wasn't anything phony or fake about what I believed. They knew that wasn't ever going to change. I never judged them or tried to be their *"spiritual policeman;"* that wasn't my job. I leave that to God. I was just me ...and tried to let *my life* be a light to them. They knew that God was first in my life ...and still is! They seldom agreed with me but they always respected and appreciated my point of view. And when real life issues took a turn for the worse they would always call on me for prayer.

I wasn't then and never have been enamored with Hollywood or celebrities; but maybe that's why we hit it off - because they weren't either. I learned about them too. With Dan I realized that Hollywood was just a natural part of his life but fame comes with a price. With "Wild Bill" I discovered that you really can't *"judge a book by its cover."* In fact, I got a real education.

I was already taking some criticism from some of the church folk. Some thought that I shouldn't be *hanging out* with that *crowd*. At the same time I was watching "Wild Bill" demonstrate some business characteristics that every preacher should be teaching to his church. I was truly beginning to get an education about human complexity and how easy it is to miss the fascinating good in people if we just live by our pre-conceived judgments.

I learned a lot about Dan that week too. In so many ways he really is that wonderful soft spoken character that he played on the Grizzly Adams TV show. It wasn't the *"script"* – it was the personality of Dan Haggerty that magically brought James Adams to life. His big smile and infectious laughter is real, it's not an act, he really does love people and he loves life. But he's a *"Pirate"* too! He's like one of the romantic versions of yesteryear. He loves pirates and he often acts like one. He's a "wild child," carefree and always sailing toward the next adventure! He's certainly not big on playing by the rules either - unless he's the one making them up!

The *Preacher, the Pirate, and the Pagan* has to be the strangest threesome in history but I'm so thankful that I have been a part of it. As you will soon see, the stories have been amazing, the friendship is incredible and the memories will be eternal.

Terry W. Bomar

Away We Go

A few events turned into more than I can remember. Every few weeks it was another airplane, a new city, the same old booth and lots of laughs; and sometimes some very strange people.

"You can't make this stuff up!" is the phrase that comes to mind. When you're traveling with a pirate, just getting there is an adventure. If the charity or event couldn't afford the first class tickets - that was no problem. The beard, the big smile, a few laughs and an autographed photo became our *magic key* to an upgrade. It wouldn't be long before Dan was *"holding court"* in first class. The economy cabin must have thought that the airlines had merged with a comedy club and *"opening night"* was being held in the front of the plane. The flight attendants and passengers were rolling with laughter as Dan would turn the trip into mile-high party central. The lay-overs weren't too bad either as long as the airport had an executive club; because I was with a pirate that had a *"magic key!"*

We wouldn't always fly; sometimes we made the mistake and drove together. On one of our early trips I decided that since it was "only" a nine hour ride - let's just drive. Dan never has been fond of long drives but this time we both thought it might be fun. We wouldn't have felt that way if we knew about the storm that was waiting for us just 90 minutes away. Not all storms are caused by the weather; and there was a big one about to hit. In less than two hours we couldn't see the road or anything else. It was a torrential downpour that had cars stopped all along the highway. We crept along hoping to get through it but that wasn't going to happen. After six hours of solid rain we weren't even halfway, and there was no let-up in sight. It was a miserable twelve hours before we finally pulled into the Hilton Hotel in South Carolina. We were exhausted; but at least our rooms were waiting for us. The event manager even left a note for us to put all our meals and needs on our room, because everything was covered. That was music to our ears because that's just what we needed, a nice steak dinner and a good night's rest.

After a big breakfast we headed to the State fairgrounds. It was a beautiful day! We welcomed the sunshine as we laid out Dan's pictures and the Young Adventurer T-shirts in the booth. Our sponsor was the owner of the giant "monster truck" that was sitting right beside our booth. He was charging to take people on wild monster truck rides all day long. The huge wheels were taller than the booth; and when he cranked it up the ground would shake. Every few minutes he would go roaring off in the field with another load with people.

People were lining up in both directions. Those in our line were waiting to get an autograph with Dan; and the other line was waiting to get a ride on the monster truck.

We knew it was going to be an interesting day when the first few people had more hair on their faces then Dan did. And some of them were women! We were way out in "the country" and I thought Dan would be a big hit – and he was! Most of the people were great, but some of them looked like they just stepped out of a *"Deliverance"* movie. Some of the other folks must have been drinking some bad moonshine.

I just loved it when the little old ladies would come up and say to Dan, *"I watched you when I was a little girl..."* Dan didn't appreciate my humor. Some of the folks reached out and pulled his beard saying: *"are you REALLY him, I thought you died? You're one of those impersonator people aren't ya?"*

One lady was so adamant that he was a fake, I said sarcastically: *"yes ma'am, that's what we do. We take fake pictures all around the country lying to people because we thought it would be fun..."*

She walked away satisfied thinking that she had proved her point. But! ...the question that never failed to make us both howl with laughter was when someone would stand 10 feet away from a giant wheel towering above them and squinting from the exhaust fumes and having to holler to speak over the roaring engine and ask:

"where can I find the monster truck ride?"
...You just can't make this stuff up!

When the two days were over we were ready to go home. We certainly weren't looking forward to that nine hour drive; but after another nice meal at the Hilton we decided to hit the road. On the road I tried to call the event manager to thank him for the wonderful accommodations. I wanted to let him know that the rooms he put us in where great and all the meals in the Hilton were fabulous; but I couldn't reach him and figured he was busy.

It wasn't an hour before ... (you guessed it) it started to rain again; and two hours later, it was still raining. This time at least we could talk as we drove because the storm wasn't blowing us off the road. However, the little rain storm outside the car wasn't near as bad as the storm that was brewing inside the car.

We started talking and discussing a few touchy issues. The conversation turned toward choices, morals and then religion. But this conversation wouldn't be like the others. Both of us dug in to our positions. I seldom ever quote scriptures when I talk because it just isn't my style. But that day we must have pushed each other's buttons because - it was on!

We talked, debated and argued for the next four hours through that driving rain. He ticked me off and I was rattling off scriptures like a machine gun. He held his own and fired his arguments right back at me. Finally he blurted out,

"pull this car over and I'm gonna beat your ass ...right here in the rain!"

I replied as dryly as I could:
"...hey man I don't want to get wet!"

We both started laughing …and we've laughed about it ever since.

When we got home, we found out that the promoter was a con-man and ripped everyone off. He never paid the fairgrounds for his event and he skipped town without paying the Hilton for our rooms and all those meals. It took a while but we finally got him in court because we weren't the only ones he burned. I'm not sure where he parks his monster truck these days; but most likely it's in the correctional center parking lot.

On another trip, this time he flew and I drove; and all the finances were taken care of in advance. It was with some wonderful people in the hills of eastern Tennessee. They wanted everything to be perfect because this was the first time they would meet the real *Grizzly Adams*. They picked out a beautiful cabin in the mountains just for him; but it didn't sound perfect when I got the call from Dan.

*"I'm gonna get for this Bomar!
You really did it to me this time!"*

I started to chuckle but I had no idea what he was talking about.
"You've got me so far out here in the woods; the squirrels are scared to be here! The driver just dropped me off here and left!

*...where are you? It's so dark out here
I saw an Owl with a flashlight!"*

When I got there a few hours later I couldn't believe it! I still laugh about it even now. These people went all-out to find the best cabin befitting their honored guest from the wilderness – *Grizzly Adams.* They purposely searched for the cabin that was the deepest one in the forest! They didn't see Dan as an actor that lived his entire life in the city of Los Angeles; they saw Grizzly Adams living in the woods with a bear.

It was beautiful, but it was so remote that I doubt *Ben the Bear* could've found this place! At night it was so dark you couldn't see your hand in front of your face. I'm laughing now even as I write this. It's hysterical just thinking about the two of us sitting on the porch at the *far end of the forest* in the pitch black night and listening to Dan grumble...

"way to go Bomar ...way to go..."

It was wild in another way when we went to Michigan for a golf tournament. It was fast paced and filled with three days of entertainment. Several celebrities showed up for the event. We joined David Carradine, Jesse Metcalf, Alto Reed, Kato Kaelin, Robbie Kinevel, Jim McMann and a bunch of other football stars and Indy Car drivers.

Early Friday afternoon Dan told me that we had been invited to dinner with Alto Reed. Alto is famous for being a founding member and the spectacular *Sax Man* of *Bob Seger's Silver Bullet Band.*

Dan said that someone was sending our ride about six p.m. When six o'clock came there was no car out front; and Dan was grinning: *"our ride is out back."* To my surprise a helicopter was waiting in the parking lot. In a few minutes we were soaring above Detroit in an open door helicopter and it wasn't long before we landed in Alto's front yard. After a tour of his beautiful home we all climbed aboard his Yacht for a stunning moon lite ride across the lake for dinner. It was the first time that I met Alto, but certainly not the last. Alto has been a great friend to me and to Young Adventurers through the years since that first amazing night.

On Saturday, after we finished our round of golf in the tournament we broke away just to check out the *Woodward Dream Cruise.* The *"cruise"* is a charity event that recreates the nostalgic heydays of the 50s and 60s, when youth, music and Motor City steel roamed Woodward Avenue, America's first highway. The first *Cruise* event was held in 1995, and 250,000 people participated—nearly ten times the number expected. The day we were there the crowd numbered 1.5 million!

The Woodward Dream Cruise is the world's largest one-day automotive event with over 40,000 classic cars from around the globe. It was unbelievable!

When we saw the crowd and all the cars, the booths and people *hawking* everything under the sun ...the *Pirate* had an idea! *"Let's sell some T-shirts! Young Adventurers can clean up here!"* Before I knew it, there we were pulled up on the side walk selling Young Adventurer T-Shirts signed by Grizzly Adams out of the truck of the car! After a couple of hours we were surrounded by some brothers that didn't seem like they were too interested in T-shirts – so we moved on. Then we spotted some other celebs signing autographs in a nice covered booth with refreshments and a fan; so the Pirate and I hijacked it! We talked our way in and sat down and sold everything we had - *"Shiva me timbers! ...Argh!!!"*

It was time to go, our work was done. We were out of T-Shirts and it was getting dark. The problem was that a million other people had the same idea. It was hopeless, we were gonna be stuck in this traffic jam for hours! It was bumper to bumper traffic. When I inched my Subaru rental car slowly past a motorcycle cop, the pirate went to work again. He rolled the window down and started talking. The conversation ended up with the cop saying:

"hey, aren't you Grizzly Adams?"

Dan said *"yeah, is there any way that we can get out this traffic jam?"*

The cop said: *"yeah, you got any pictures?"* And just like that ...the magic key worked again!

The officer flipped on the siren, started moving cars and soon we were driving on the sidewalks, through crowds of people and past the traffic jams. When we hit the highway, for the first time in my life, I had a cop pull to my window while I was driving as fast as I could, and yell *"can't you go any faster?"* I told him I had it floored and I would try to keep up!

With the lights flashing and sirens blaring he escorted us to the outer edge of Detroit and pulled into the "Y" where two highways split. And once again there we were ...in between two highways

with cars zooming by at eighty miles an hour, in the middle of the night with Dan signing pictures on the hood of the car! I was just mumbled:
> "Way to go Dan ...way to go..."

The Michigan trip ended with a couple of laughs. My last day there was Sunday, so I found a church and went to the morning service. Just as the service was ending my phone rings with the voice of my friendly pirate on the other end. *"Where are you?" "I'm in church!" I replied.* He said with a sinister chuckle, *"Well I'm at the Michigan NASCAR 400!"* To which I blurted out (in church mind you) *"Wait a minute! ...how can I get there?"* He just laughed and laughed and never let me hear the end of it!

Before we parted ways on Monday *"Pirate Black Beard"* had one more trick up his sleeve. As I left the hotel I asked him and Bill where I should leave the brand new golf clubs the event had given me to use in the tournament? They said: *"Oh no Rev., those were a gift to all the celebrities for being in the tournament!"*

> **Note:** Never trust a Pirate named, Grizzly!

Naïve me ...I said "Awesome!" and headed to the airport for Florida; Dan and Bill left for Los Angeles. A couple of days later I got a call ...and you'll never guess who it was from - Wink!

The summer of strangeness was far from over. We had one more shot to raise some money for Young Adventurers. It would be in Orlando and our last stop in the *T-Shirts on Tour*. This was a combination outdoor sportsman and rugged furniture show. This time I had an idea.

I have been a sportsman all my life (I told you that Dan and I were opposites). My favorite sportsman was Teddy Roosevelt. He loved hunting and fishing all over the world, but it is because of his love for the sport that we have the national parks system today. Like me and most sportsmen, he loved hunting, fishing and the outdoors and wanted everyone to enjoy it.

Every year for over two decades I've spent time in Alaska hunting, fishing, rafting, camping and climbing mountains. One year I killed a huge grizzly bear that stands mounted in my office.

I thought it would be funny to have him standing by the booth when Dan signed the autographs – at least it would draw more attention. After Dan left in a car for Orlando I borrowed a small pick-up and strapped the bear into the back *"standing up"* looking over the cab of the truck.

When I caught up to Dan and pulled alongside of his car; I thought he was going to run off the road laughing. But as funny as that was, it was just the beginning.

Arriving at the Orlando Hilton with Grizzly Adams
...interesting.

Walking through the Hilton pushing a Grizzly Bear
...hilarious.

Surprising an eighty year old lady
when the elevator doors open
...PRICELESS!

Terry W. Bomar

A New Tour Begins

While we were in Orlando we made some new contacts that totally changed our course; at least for a while. Following in the steps of Cindy Crawford and Jaclyn Smith; Dan combined his passion and talent into designing a furniture and accessory collection and launched Dan Haggerty's *Grizzly Adams* Wildlife Collection.

It wasn't long before we were on tour again. This time it was all about promoting the new furniture line. Dan had schlepped all over the place to help Young Adventurers; now it was my turn to travel to assist him. We traveled to all the major furniture shows in North Carolina, Atlanta, Dallas, Denver and Tupelo just to name a few.

At the first show we joined Jaclyn Smith who was promoting her line as well. She was on one floor and we were on another. Even the NASCAR King Richard Petty showed up for an appearance. The show was great, but I can't say much for the rest of it. The company CEO was a nice guy "sorta;" but on the first trip we realized how "careful" he was with money.

He was proud to have a celebrity with him and said he wanted to take us all out for a nice dinner. Oh course my mind goes back to Hollywood and The Bistro Gardens. Hey, I figured if a southern preacher had enough class to swallow an $800 dollar check, then this dinner was going to be fabulous since he was a millionaire!

When we pulled up to *The Golden Corral* ...Dan snickered *"you've got to be kidding me..."* As I watched Dan politely stand behind a sweet old lady with his plate in hand to pick up some southern fried chicken ...it was everything I could do to get from falling on the floor in hysterics! I'm laughing now!

As funny as that was, there was more to come. We were told that they had a "suite" reserved for Dan during the three day event. He omitted the part about the "suite" being in a home he had rented for his entire crew. To top that off, he expected me and Dan to share it! THAT ...wasn't about to happen!

The only problem was that it was during the furniture season and ALL the hotels in town were booked solid. We were stuck. So, I found some kids room in the house and hijacked that one and left Dan in his "suite;" aka the bedroom on the top floor. Actually we always "try" to be "nice guys" about this stuff but sharing a house with a dozen people was really pushing the limits. We NEVER let that happen again!

After that experience, we had to hold a hard line on the flights and accommodations. We decided to watch everything to make sure we didn't end up having to fly — *holding on the wing!*

> **Note:** Some millionaires are a LOT more carless with your comfort then they are with their own.

(That's another thing I liked about *"Wild Bill."* He was always as classy and generous to you as he was to himself. How's that for the "Golden Rule" — and from an ex-con no less!)

After that cozy experience in the "frat house hotel" we laid down the requirements before Dan ever traveled to another show again. This wasn't about celebrity (Dan's not like that), this was about respect. After all, anyone who has ever seen him in action at a tradeshow knows that Dan is a fabulous promoter! Unfortunately this kind of thing happens often to celebrities after the *"new wears off"* and the company tries to cut as many corners as possible.

The furniture circuit was actually quite fun; but the differences were growing. Dan continually wanted to upgrade the line to custom high class designs but "Mr Careful" was determined to stay with those made in China. I understood both sides, but I could see the writing on the wall.

What happened next didn't help at all. We arrived for the Denver show at midnight; it was cold and the pick-up person was nowhere in sight. We tried to laugh it off when we hired a car service and the driver could barely speak English and obviously knew nothing about getting around Denver. He was either lost or just trying to scam us, but we weren't in the mood. After a few minutes of threatening to make him move over and let us drive, he finally dropped us at the Hotel. At least the rooms were okay but I knew this wasn't good for anyone.

We always had fun at the shows because all the other exhibitors loved Dan being there; and they were constantly giving us stuff. By now you should know that Dan and I are extremely competitive with each other. The tradeshow *getting stuff* was a challenge! After all he was famous, and he has years of experience being a Pirate too! I'm just a lowly Tennessee preacher trying to make it through this cruel world. I must say that I didn't often win but I kept the race close. He would come back to our booth with a new shirt and I would come back with two new shirts. I would land some teddy bear and he would get a bigger one – you get the idea.

One day I found a little *"Teddy Bear in a Can"* that was so cute I had to have it for my little girl. I started with the most charming lines in my arsenal. I figured I can do this; they don't call me *"golden tongue"* for nothing! I enjoyed it thoroughly when I came back to our booth victorious waving my *"Teddy Bear in a Can"* at Dan with a triumphant giggle. He just ignored me. When I got home my little girl came running up to me saying:

"Daddy what did you bring me?"
and I proudly pulled out my *"Teddy Bear in a Can."*

"but Daddy ...there's nothing in the can..."

Argh!!! ...The Pirate Strikes again!

One of the best things that came from the furniture line was when the three of us (Me, Dan and Wild Bill) opened the new store on Palm Beach Island. It was a beautiful store in the wealthiest zip code in

America, just a mile or two from Donald trump's home and private club Mar-A-Lago.

It was perfect because it had a showroom for the furniture down stairs and offices for the Young Adventurers charity offices up stairs. Palm Beach is the charity fundraising capital of the world. There is a charity ball or event every night on *"the island"* during the *"season."*

> Let's get this straight; a beautiful location,
> lots of parties and powerful people –
> the perfect place for a Pirate!

We opened the new store with a big party in December, and called it *Beyond Decor*. It was full of furniture and accessories that were appropriate for the Palm Beach crowd. We focused on a lot of Art, high-end accessories and some antiques as well. It was the first time Dan had been to *"the island"* but they all knew him and showed up for the Grand Opening. My kids would run the store downstairs and I would run Young Adventurers upstairs. Everything was good; but of course it wasn't long before the pirate would make things a little more interesting.

Dan had his film and television work in Hollywood and Bill lived in Long Beach. They would pop over for all the celebrity events as much as they could.

The Life and Times of Dan Haggerty

Dan and his wife Sam; came over with Bill and his wife Cindy came over for a week during the Grand Opening.

It was a Friday evening when the terrible

> **Note:** It may be dangerous to allow a Pirate and a Pagan to run loose together unsupervised on Palm Beach Island.

twosome came strolling into the store demanding that I go with them. I was busy greeting guests ...during the Grand Opening weekend mind you! But they insisted that I go with them; so I left. Driving south on Ocean I watched the waves and wondered to myself ...what has he got me into this time?

I had no clue! *"Where are we going I demanded?"* I had lived in Florida for twenty years and I knew Palm Beach. We were in the *"really high rent district."* Dan said that earlier in the day he and Bill were just driving around when he had to use the restroom and he pulled into one of the drives ...and they let him in! He said:

"Terry you've gotta see this house!" I burst out *"are you kidding me? You dragged me away from the store to show me the place where you went to pee? You can't be serious!"*

Then he pulled into the driveway.

"You didn't! You can't do this!"

He did! Out of ALL the homes in Palm Beach he could've chosen ...this pirate rolled up to Donald Trump's door and asked:
"can I use your potty?"
REALLY!!!

Now, he's dragging me back as a witness to this embarrassing craziness.

"Hey Dan! Remember ... I've got to LIVE HERE!"

He pulls up to the door of Mar-a-Lago as I am sliding into the back floorboard. The doorman comes running out...

"Mr Haggerty! Come on in,
we're so glad you came back!

So Bill and I step out the car like diplomats. Two feet into the door he already has everyone's attention. They're laughing and snapping pictures as Bill and I are just grinning.

"You guys are staying for the party, right?
You know Diana Ross will be here to sing –
you guys can't leave!"

We didn't!

Of this one thing I am certain about Dan Haggerty, you NEVER know what's gonna happen next. One minute I'm slumping into the floorboard of a the back seat; the next minute I'm sitting by the pool at Mar-a-Lago.

The waiters were dropping off drinks and appetizers while we enjoyed the private party and evening music under a beautiful South Florida sky.

Sometimes it's nice to know a Pirate!

Terry W. Bomar

The Life and Times of Dan Haggerty

Trumped!

The Mar-a-Lago restroom run turned party central was just the beginning of a long and interesting friendship the Donald.

The name Mar-A-Lago is Spanish for "Sea to Lake". It was designed by Joseph Urban and built in 1924-1927, by Marjorie Merriweather Post with her (then) husband, Edward F. Hutton. When she died in 1973 Marjorie Post willed the 17-acre estate to the U.S. Government as a retreat for Presidents and visiting foreign dignitaries. In what many at the time thought was an ill-advised move, Donald bought the 126-room, 110,000-square-foot estate for about $10 million for the estate in 1985 to create the Mar-A-Lago Club. After acquiring the property, Trump had the property renovated, with 58 bedrooms, 33 bathrooms, a 29-foot long marble top dining table, 12 fireplaces, and three bomb shelters. Also, the home has five clay and one grass tennis court with a waterfront pool. Recently he added a 20,000-square-foot ballroom with a multi-million dollar gold leaf ceiling.

The Donald knew what he was doing. Today, Mar-a-Lago is one of the finest and most prestigious clubs in all of America, with a "Six Star" rating. It is the premiere place for the finest charity events on the island.

In 1994, Michael Jackson and Lisa Marie Presley spent their honeymoon at Mar-a-Lago. Donald's spectacular club has received Diplomats, Presidents,

Entertainers and Celebrities; but now he is entertaining a pirate, and of course Dan would make the best of it.

After the Christmas concert party had ended and all the guests were gone, Dan was still having fun cutting up with the staff. On our way out, as we walked through the magnificent living room toward the entrance, I pointed out a beautiful poinsettia.

It was huge, the biggest I had ever seen. As Bill and I chatted outside and waited for the valet to bring the car around we noticed that Dan was nowhere to be found. As the valet handed me the keys I got into the driver's seat and here comes Dan – carrying that giant poinsettia.

"Pop the truck, hurry this thing is heavy!"

I did; and he put the plant in the trunk and off we went. I was afraid to ask, so I didn't. I didn't want to know if he talked them out of it ...or just collected a souvenir; so I gave him *the look.*
But with a swashbuckler grin he said,

> *"What? ...You needed a nice plant
> and he had a lot of them..."*

Later that year I would once again cross paths with the Trumps; when a gentleman walked into the store to buy one of our antique lamps. Little did I know that it was Donald's brother-in-law. He wanted as many of the lamps as I could get my hands on. Soon I was touring the construction site of his and Elizabeth Trump's new home. Jim had very specific tastes and he wanted the bronze lamps to place around the outside of his home.

In the process Jim and I became close friends and I spent many evenings dining with him and Elizabeth. Jim and Elizabeth are two of the nicest people I have ever met. Elizabeth has that Trump style and class that she carries with a very humble and kind personality.

I'll never forget the time we were scheduled to go to dinner together but I was too sick to get out of bed. It wasn't long before I heard a knock at my door and they came walking in to personally dropped off a complete dinner so I wouldn't *"skip eating."*

But things in the furniture world still weren't going too well. There was a continuing friction of styles between Dan and the owner of the company and the upcoming Las Vegas show would bring everything to a boil. The owner spent thousands on the booth and preparation for the show but decided to skimp again on Dan. This time he didn't ask, he just informed us that we "would" be staying at the cheaper hotel and we would share a room, *"no questions asked, we had no choice in the matter."*

I tried to explain that this wasn't the best way to handle this; and it certainly was going to go well with *Grizzly Black Beard the Pirate.*

Note: *"When two elephants start fighting ...it's always the grass that suffers the most!"*

I tried to be the peace maker but it was no use. Dan didn't show up for the event and I flew out to Vegas to try and change his mind. I figured that at least I would showed up to help out at the booth; but that was it, It was over!

Both of these hard heads refused to budge; and I would soon be the one to suffer. In a few weeks a truck pulled up outside our store and they loaded up all the furniture that we had on consignment. He was my furniture supplier and everything that wasn't paid for they hauled away. But what seemed bad at the moment turned into a blessing. With the furniture gone, I turned it into *Beyond Art Gallery*.

It wasn't long before we were having weekly parties, charity events for Young Adventurers and artist showings from all over America. I even held church services in there on Sundays; it was fabulous!

As my friendship grew with Jim and Elizabeth, I spent a lot more time at Mar-a-Lago. The first time I personally met Donald Trump was at his lavish New Year's Eve party that was attended by the likes of Rod Stewart, Regis Philbin, and many more.

I must say, forget what you've heard ...he really is a nice person. That wouldn't be the last New Year's party or the last time I would see Mar-a-Lago.

Jim took me on a tour of the entire place and we often ate lunch there together. Jim and Elizabeth helped with my charity and over the next few years we held several Young Adventurer events at the Mar-a-Lago Club.

The greatest of these events were the *"Out of Africa"* Safari Balls that were always "wild" and always fun! Everyone came in *Safari Sheik* and the dinner was some wild form of surf and turf; the music was exotic, the décor was extreme, and it complete with fiery torches' and live animals! Actress Shelly Long joined us and of course, Grizzly Adams showed up to bring some added excitement.

Terry W. Bomar

The Life and Times of Dan Haggerty

Wild Bill

Someone once told me: *"Don't judge someone else just because their sins are different than yours."*

I certainly think that it applies to my friend *"Wild Bill"Stallings.* Make no mistake, he would be the first to say that he had lived a wild and sinful life. Perhaps he was even proud of it. In his early life he really was wild; I didn't know him until he was in his seventies and I still saw his wild streak from time to time. I just made it a point that anytime that he and the pirate got too crazy for me, I would find somewhere else to be.

I always try to look a little deeper than just our differences or outward behaviors. I figured that since the Bible says that *God looks on the heart,* that's what I wanted to do too. I am so glad that I did; because under that rough and rugged exterior I discovered a kind and man. He was like a sweet old grandfather that always had a smile and something positive to say.

That's the man I knew, but there was a much darker side too. Bill's early years started like so many people in the sixties; they were filled with sex, drugs and rock n' roll. Those weren't just a few events; they were a way of life. When he entered the culture of Hollywood everything just intensified. He played in several western "B-movies" and even starred in several commercials as *"The Marlboro Man."* He was deep into the drug culture and dealing was just part of it. He spent seven years in prison for counterfeiting. Grand larceny, grand theft and a lot of violence were all part of the game. He spent years as loan shark and an enforcer for the motorcycle gang. He was married seven times (at last count) and yet, most of them are still friends ...I think?

We had many conversations about all of those things. I'm still not sure how he compartmentalized it all. By the time I knew him he was well into his seventies. I never actually saw it ...but the common knowledge was that if there was a party, Bill would be the last one to leave – the next day. You could see the *"hard living"* in his face and hear it in his words; but he was never a vulgar or abusive kind of person.

However, it was very easy to see (and feel) that this was not a guy to *mess with.* The only time I ever saw that happen was in a limo. Dan, Bill and I were joined with famed Chicago Bear's Super Bowl Quarterback Jim McMann , Kato Kaelin, some other guests and "Saved by the Bell's - Mr. Belding."

We all could tell fairly quickly that Bill and Belding rubbed each other the wrong way. No one is really sure what happened, but before that ride was over something was said; and the next I knew we were pulling Bill off the guy! I don't know who started it, but you can be sure that *"Mr. Belding"* was *"Saved by the Bell"* on that one!

I am not saying that good behavior one day condones bad behavior the next; and I'm sure that Bill would agree. What I found interesting about Bill was the kinder gentler side of him. Dan said that as long as he knew Bill he would always share his good fortune anytime things were going well. Dan recalled a time when Bill threw a bunch of furs on the bed and said *"pick out a couple and take them home to Samantha"* (Dan's wife).

I often knew of Bill helping some young person get started in business, or buying nice gifts for people for no reason; and he was unique in the way he helped people. When someone was in trouble and went to him for help he never questioned them or scold them for getting into to trouble - he either helped or he didn't. If he trusted you he would, but if he didn't trust you he wouldn't. Those that asked for a gift, either got it or they didn't; but if they asked for a loan he expected them to pay it back on time. It was all about respect with him.

Bill, Dan and I were in Hawaii together at *The Turtle Bay Resort* sitting by the pool when he began questioning me about Young Adventurers. He wanted to know what our plans were for the future and what we were doing at the moment. I told him all about the kids and my attempts to get them to *stretch their vision.* He loved the idea. I explained that we were like Big Brothers and Big Sisters that taught kids to build their integrity and life vision. Our goal is to create in them the courage to not only reach for their dreams; but how to take the steps to achieve them.

The current project we were working on was a video series using adventure to teach character. At the time we had just taken kids to Ft Lauderdale to dive with the legendary Oceanographer *Jean-Michel Cousteau* and release sharks back out into the wild. Bill got excited and told everyone that they needed to talk to me; it was very encouraging.

Three days after I got home from Hawaii, a package came to the door. There was a letter taped to the outside of the package. I opened the letter that read:

"Thanks Rev for all you do; God has been merciful to me and I just wanted to help out with your video."

I was excited that somehow *"maybe"* my actions and my life *"just may"* have had a small part in causing this man who at first declared that he didn't believe in anything to now say that God had been merciful to him.

I must admit that it didn't take me long to read the letter and immediately start tearing into the package. I had to sit down for minute to catch my breath ...because when I opened the package...

...ten thousand dollars in cash fell on the floor!

That's the way Bill was ...no fanfare just do it.

He never even mentioned it again after that day; but he did enjoy the video that he funded. The gifts weren't always large, some were small and personal; like the gold cross he and Dan bought for me in New Orleans when Dan was Grand Marshall of the Mardi Gras Parade. He did the same thing for many people for many reasons. Dan has spoken often about how many times Bill would get involved in one film project or some deal he had going. Bill was always there in good times and bad. He even got involved when Dan and I were creating *Dan Haggerty's Wild Adventures in Tennessee*. It was to be a three million dollar wildlife park to teach young people about exotic animals and serve as an exotic animal rescue. Unfortunately our hopes were crushed when the Tennessee tornados and the clean-up afterward forced the City to withdraw from the project.

But as I said ...good deeds don't erase bad behavior and some of Bill's old chickens would soon come home to roost. He was in his late seventies when some things came out of the past and threatened to send him back to prison. He handled it in the same "matter of fact" manner he handled everything else. He said *"if it happens it happens. I am going to fight the best I can but it is what is."*

I never pried into his business for details; the three of us always held that type of respect and boundaries. If he wanted to tell me he would; he didn't. What I do know is that because of the time that had gone by and his age, they were able to plead it down to a year in jail and probation. So he held a party and reported to prison the next day.

The Life and Times of Dan Haggerty

When he got out it wasn't long before he too would fight for his life against cancer. By the time they had a diagnosis ...it was stage 4 lung cancer. There was little hope but he fought it hard and still lived his life. His last trip was with Dan They hopped in the car and drove to Tijuana Mexico to relive some of the good times they used to have there watching the sunset. I spent a lot of time with him too.

The last time the three of us were together was on New Year's Eve. It was a nice time I won't forget. Over the next few months the cancer got worse. I spent a lot of time and phone calls with Bill to pray with him. Dan was there every day to make him feel better until our friend left us.

"Wild Bill" died in the spring.
But he didn't die a Pagan!

Terry W. Bomar

The Life and Times of Dan Haggerty

Castles, Boats & Bears

For a while life slipped into a routine that we had not been used too for quite some time. Dan was involved in the Resort Industry as a long term spokesman. It took up a lot of his time. I was busy with the Art Gallery, Young Adventurers and preaching around the country. I still managed some of the projects but there wasn't a lot to manage.

There was an entire nation between us and we figured at least we would get along better that way - wink. We still did a few shows and events together but the heavy touring had died down; and we both needed it. We had both tired a little from all the crazy requests like the sponsor that wanted him to ride a buffalo and sing while wearing a coon-skin cap and rawhide jacket. Trust me – he didn't do it!

Dan continued to appear in several films and Hollywood projects and I was involved in a few of them as well. In fact, I even got him to do Christian Faith Based film called *The Book of Ruth, A Journey of Faith.* It was a nice little project that I talked him into doing for a friend; and besides, I was to work in the film too. I thought that it would be fun and it was; but we had more fun off the set than on it.

We were on location in the tiny town of Eureka Springs, Arkansas and one day we took off to go "exploring," which Dan loves to do. With a population of a little more than 2000, Eureka Springs is a unique Victorian resort village. The city has steep winding streets filled with Victorian-style cottages and manors. The streets curve around the hills and rise and fall with the topography in a five-mile loop. Eureka Springs is sometimes called *The Little Switzerland of America* because of its mountainous terrain and the winding, up-and-down paths of its streets and walkways. The streets wind around the town and no two roads intersect at a 90 degree angle; so there are no traffic lights.

We met incredibly interesting people and artists in town but quest had just begun. Dan even found his old buddy *Willie Nelson* nearby and spent some time with him in the bus. On the way back to the set we noticed on the skyline what look like a castle!

Well, if you know Dan you know that he is intrigued by Castles, Dragons, Vikings and the Renaissance. He immediately yelled,
"Let's go check that out!"

So off we went trying to weave our way through the mountains until we finally found the long driveway up to the massive castle.

It's called *Castle Rogue's Manor* and is over 15,000 sq. ft. of pure architectural fantasy. It is situated on 20 acres of Ozark forest only six miles from Eureka Springs. The Castle sits on the cliffs overlooking the White River & Table Rock Lake that provides spectacular views. It took the owner over 16 years to design and build this unbelievable castle in the sky. When we got to the massive door no one was home; but that's no problem for a pirate!

He checked the door and when he found it open, he just walked on in! I was screaming at him,

"... Dude, are you nuts! We're gonna get shot!"

> **Note:** *"Pirates that are obsessed with Castles and happen to find one wide open and unoccupied – are hard of hearing!"*

He never looked look back; we explored every inch the place while I kept calling out *"is anybody home?"*

After an hour or so, he decided to head for town and look for the owner. I figured that since I got out of that place with my life in tack, I didn't want to push our luck. The last person I wanted to see …was the owner! But sure enough we found him …and they became the best of friends.

The owner was Smith Treuer, whose worldwide travels and love of art and history sparked his creative genius to build this magnificent Castle on the river.

I just smiled and thought how glad I was that this pirate was on my side!

When the film wrapped, he went back to LA and I went back to Palm Beach. He was busy with more film projects and promoting two Orlando Resorts.

I was busy with Young Adventurers. That summer we held the *Pirates of the Caribbean Adventure.*

We took several kids from the United States to join some Caribbean kids sailing in the Bahama Out Islands.

The next year's adventure was a Father/Son trip to the Wilderness of the Wrangle Mountains in Alaska. Dan couldn't make it on the Pirate trip; but I wasn't about to let him miss this one. It had *Grizzly Adams* written all over it.

It was the *Great Adventure to the Great Land*, as Alaska is often called. We took several adults and kids on the ten day adventure deep into Alaska's Wrangle Mountains. The wilderness wasn't so bad but the first leg of the trip was.

We landed in Fairbanks and had to squeeze everyone into a 15 passenger van for a several hour

> **Note:** This may be a good place to reiterate how much Dan hates long car rides.

trip through the winding mountain roads to Tok, Alaska. Needless to say, it will be a few more decades before he forgives me...

In Tok, we all boarded three single engine Cessna's for the flight into our remote lodge. We would spend the next few days with a real Mountain Man named

Terry Overly, the owner of *Pioneer Outfitters*. Terry has spent his entire life in the wild *Wrangle Mountain Range.*

When we arrived Terry and his staff treated us to his first class "5 Star wilderness" lodge. It was rugged but awesome. Every building was made of logs and built by hand (mostly Terry Overly's hands).

The Life and Times of Dan Haggerty

The only way in or out was by bush plane or horseback. The mornings started with the smell of coffee and a big Alaskan breakfast in the main house. The day would end while we sat by the fire outside our personal cabins.

Even the hot tube and steam room were heated by real fresh cut wood in the furnace.

We explored an abandoned gold mine and glacier from the air by Bush Plane and on the ground by horseback. We spent days camping in the magnificent mountain ranges.

When it was time to leave, we all left by horseback; everyone but Dan.

We left him behind to wait for a ride on the Bush Plane. After all he was the celebrity... wink.

In Alaska during the summer months, the sun doesn't set until approx. midnight. We were tired and it was getting dark as we rode into camp after crossing icy rivers and some of the most beautiful scenery you've ever seen.

The Life and Times of Dan Haggerty

Finally, we heard the sound of the Bush plane flying overhead. That sound meant that our pirate would be arriving any minute.

When Dan walked in, he was shaking his head and telling (what I thought was) a funny story. He told us that after we rode off leaving him all alone in the camp; he sat for hours waiting for the bush plane. In the "bush," it's easy for the plane to be delayed.

We left him with a rifle because we were in thick grizzly country. After a while he thought it might be wise to check the gun. When he did he realized that the gun was fine but someone left the wrong shells!

We started laughing and reminded him that he didn't need bullets – he was Grizzly Adams!
   ...and we laughed and laughed.

Terry W. Bomar

The Life and Times of Dan Haggerty

A Real World Education

As a minister, counselor and student of sociology; people have been my business all my life.

I'm so thankful for the unique perspective I've been afforded by my profession, my education and the wonderfully strange life experiences I've gained as a member of *the Preacher, the Pirate, and the Pagan trio.*

I've had annual *"season tickets"* to witness the drama of two very different extremes from the church world to Hollywood; and learn from the mixture of two very different personalities with my own. The education I received far outweighs anything I could've learned in a classroom.

I gained an enormous appreciation for people and positions far different from my own. I have witnessed up close and personally the deep seated needs common to us all; regardless of our personal, political or religious positions. Unfortunately I have also been grieved to watch good people refuse honest dialogue choosing rather to barricade themselves safely behind their stone walled ideologies and hurl judgments at the other side. And fortunately, I have been blessed to see some of the best attributes in humanity in the most uncommon places. But most of all I am amazed at how much deeper my faith has grown as I have tried to see everyone through the eyes of God.

I realized that I never have to compromise my beliefs in any circumstance; nor do I have to hold others accountable to the principles that I've chosen for myself, in order to be friends.

One of my favorite experiences came when Dan and I were attending the premiere of a movie he had recently completed. It had all the usual trappings starting with the red carpet, limos and lights. After the film all celebrities were signing autographs before they heading to the premiere party that followed.

The party was crowded with celebrities and guests all enjoying the banquet of food and drinks; along with live music, lights and dancing. While I enjoyed myself, I thought about those that would recite their favorite criticisms of me for being there. But my thought was,

"Where else should I be?"

A few minutes later a well-known television celebrity walked up and asked to speak with me.

> *"Can you help me? Can you do with me what you've obviously done with Dan?"*

I had no idea what he was talking about?

> *"What do you mean, I'm not an agent?"*

Agitated he replied:

> *"No, no, no …I'm not talking about movies! I'm talking about God! He said that you are an Ordained Minister. …Can you help me?"*

Stunned …I said:
> *"Of course I can…"*

And with that, the next thing I knew we were in his hotel room talking and praying for three hours! A few months later he received devastating news on a career matter. We met a few more times because he was determined to turn to God rather than back to drugs and alcohol like he used to do.

It was living proof that people everywhere, every day, in every walk of life are hungry for truth, guidance and meaning. I am so grateful that I could be there *as a vessel* in his time of trouble.

> *Like I said before …where else should I be?*

Through the years, I also saw the hypocrisy and ugliness of Hollywood ...and of Grizzly Adams.

My first surprising experience came when I met *Charles E. Sellier Jr.;* who wrote the novel that eventually became the film and television show that we know as *The Life and Times of Grizzly Adams.*

Known to most as *"Chuck,"* he was nice enough to me but when the subject of *Grizzly Adams* came up he became immediately obsessive, almost paranoid.

It was obvious that he had a great deal of insecurity and jealousy because of the fame and popularity Dan had acquired. Everyone, even to this day recognizes that Dan Haggerty is the *face* of *Grizzly Adams*; but Chuck just couldn't handle it.

Despite the desires of millions of fans and dozens of production companies that wanted more Grizzly Adams type films, Chuck would do anything to keep it from happening; if Dan Haggerty was involved.

The Life and Times of Dan Haggerty

I just wanted to find a way to make peace and somehow bring about an agreeable solution. From day one, Dan always wanted to be friends again with Chuck. He wanted to let their differences stay in the past; but Chuck wouldn't have any of it.

In my first conversation with Chuck he rattled off accusations at Dan like a machine gun. At the time, Chuck had no idea I was a minister with over twenty five years' experience. So when Chuck included a few scriptures to bolster his case, which was founded mostly on bitterness; he finally met someone he couldn't fool.

I led him through dozens of scriptures to remind him of forgiveness, peace, healing and love until he finally blurted out

"what do want from me?"

I replied:
"If you are what you say you are; I want you to give up your 25 year old grudge! How can you say that you love God who you cannot see; if you hate your brother who can see?"

He never quoted another scripture to me again — ever! It took a few more years and a lot more phone calls but he finally softened; but sadly he died tragically shortly thereafter.

There is far too much to tell here; but in the coming editions of this book series you will learn much more about the creators, cast and crew and all the extraordinary drama that existed behind the cameras of one of America's favorite television shows. Perhaps they should have called it...

The Lifes, Deaths, and Tragedies of Grizzly Adams.

Primarily, I've noticed how small-minded people can be; and how damaging it is for everyone - regardless of the circles they run in. In the church world it is dangerously easy to become judgmental of others and thereby lose any opportunity to share the real benefits of faith. In Hollywood it's dangerously easy to become egocentric and thereby isolate yourself from success or even worse; become so narcissistic that you wouldn't appreciate success if you found it.

One of the best times Dan, Bill and I had was at *The Golden Boot Awards* in 2004, when Val Kilmer was one of the honorees.

The Golden Boot Awards honor actors, actresses, and crew members who have made significant contributions to the genre of Western television and movies. As I said earlier that I don't get enamored with celebrities; but to be honest, that night I was impressed. We were sitting at the table with Dan and Bill's good friend Bill Smith who has starred in hundreds of films. Bill Smith, was sitting beside me and we spoke most of the evening. Not far away were some of the classic stars of yesterday like Jane Russell, and Mickey Rooney, to name a few. Val Kilmer spoke and Tommy Lee Jones who had received his award the year before was also there.

It was a great night but reality set in the next day when Dan took me to visit the Screen Actors Guild (S.A.G.) Retirement Center and Nursing Home. Dan visits there quite often. As we walked the halls Dan greeted one after another and would quietly tell me who they "were" when they were famous. It brought tears to my eyes as I spoke to them, not because of who they were; but because of who they are now. I asked Dan how often he came out,

> *"as much as I possibly can,*
> *because some of them have no one!"*

In a twenty four hour period I had gone from the glitz and glamour of a banquet to award the statue of a boot painted gold; to the stark reality of the brevity of life and that is what's really important. When we stood by the bed of his friend that was fighting for his life. Dan got us all laughing and before we left I had us all holding hands and praying. I never saw Hollywood the same again.

I never saw Dan the same again...

Terry W. Bomar

The Inside Passage

Only a few people really know what's been a major motivation for the *Inside Passage* screenplay.

Obviously, Dan has a love for the character that he made famous and for all the fans that have shown him so much love through the years. It has always been his desire to be a part of more family films.

We had begun tinkering with ideas for our own independent film. A film that would reconnect people of today with the wonders of the wilderness - in the "spirit of Grizzly Adams." In 2008, I wrote one draft after another under different titles but soon tragedy would strike - twice!

> Note: Yes, even Pirates love family!
>
> Dan, no doubt will always be seen by many as a "wild-child." But if you could see him run around his home playing with his grandson, you might realize how sincere Dan is about family and family films."

Actually *"our"* film would become a personal *Inside Passage* that Dan and I we would take together in the years to come. We have always laughed about how different our lives are; but that year brought tragic events that we would have in common for the rest of our lives.

My youngest son Hunter and I had just been to Gander Mountain to shoot our compound bows together. It was a great father and son time and we stopped in to McDonalds before heading home.

Hunter is the last of my four children. My first two children, Terry Jr., and Trinity were from my first marriage and several years older than Chelsey and Hunter, my last two kids. As Hunter stood in line to order his food, I will never forget what happened next.

My cell phone rang, and as soon as I said hello: There was silence on the other end. Then my oldest daughter's husband said:
> *"Trinity's mom passed away..."*

With those words my mind went blank – I don't remember much after that for a while. I do remember slamming the dashboard and crying so hard I couldn't see to drive. Hunter was doing his best to comfort me.

We had been married for fourteen years. And although it had been sixteen years since our marriage ended; we were the best of friends.

Now I had lost my friend, my two oldest kids, Trinity and Terry Jr., had lost their mother, Natalie had lost her grandmother, and the world had lost a wonderful woman at the tender age of 48.

I was devastated for my kids and for myself.

I travelled with them to Tennessee to participate in preaching her funeral in our hometown of Memphis. Then we returned to Florida, where I preached a memorial service for her, with all her friends in Florida.

During that tragic time, it was as though everything in the world came to a screeching halt. Nothing else was important anymore. Nothing compares to the value of life or the loss of someone you love.

The Bible so correctly describes life as a lovely wild flower in a field that *"is here today and gone tomorrow."* It appears almost magically from where or for what reason is a mystery.

It's a miracle that beautifies everything around it - simply by its existence. Life is a fragile masterpiece fashioned meticulously by the Creator for His own purpose and pleasure.

We don't own it, but we are the recipients of all its glory – and that by the gift of God.

June was a gift that God had given to us all. Her life was brief but her contribution was eternal. She was like a bouquet of flowers carefully selected and arranged by her creator.

We were simply the beneficiaries to whom God had presented this loveliness. And though her earthly life has ended; like a flower that fades in time.
When you stop and sense the stillness; the flowers may be gone but the fragrance still is mine.

Through the years I have always noticed that Dan is very sensitive in times like these – especially when it comes to his friends and family. He dropped everything when Bill was sick and dying. He spent his time just trying to make Bill's last days more comfortable – and he did.

Now it was my turn. Dan called me two or three times a day – everyday. He was truly concerned because he knew that nothing had ever affected me as deeply as June's loss.

Then one day ...he didn't call. When I called him I wasn't crying anymore – he was crying.

"Dan! What's wrong?"

Through all of his emotion he could barely whisper, *"Sam is in intensive care."*

Dan and Samantha had been together for over twenty five years and she was the *"love of his life."*

Samantha had been in a traffic accident and suffered a severe head injury.

There was little that anyone could do. Dan could only stand beside her bedside with their children and try to comfort them as they faced the inevitable - that their mom and his *beautiful Sam* was gone.

I flew to California as quickly as possible.

On August 15th I joined many other friends to honor this wonderful woman, wife and mother. I had the distinct honor of performing the memorial service for Samantha that day, which happened to also be my birthday.

In twenty four short days ...unimaginable tragedy had struck twice! Dan and I were bonded in the pain of that time that would change our lives forever.

The severe grief and fog that followed those dark days were very hard to navigate. But eventually the screenplay that I had written took on new significance. It became our needed distraction and solace. We threw ourselves into the work both creatively and functionally. Producing this film became extremely important to both of us for many reasons.

The Life and Times of Dan Haggerty

The title *Inside Passage* stuck in part because the film is based in Alaska which is the home of the southeastern sea lanes known as the Inside Passage. However, the title also reflects the theme of the film as *Jack* takes his own internal journey and transforms into the man he was meant to be.

After our own private tragedies, the project earned its title for giving us strength and purpose during our own personal *Inside Passage*.

The script received some great reviews at first and we were soon talking to three respected Directors who wanted to direct the film. That's when more tragedy struck.

Dan's close friend David Carradine, had already told us privately that he wanted to do the film and what part he wanted to play. With David's commitment we were arranging for the production funding, but on June 3, 2009 our dear friend David was found dead in Bangkok, Thailand where he was shooting his latest film, *"Stretch."* at the time.

The next twenty months became an unbelievable roller coaster of emotion because every time we reached the heights of expectation something tragic would happen.

In future editions of this book series we will talk about the double digits of deaths we've been through in the process of making this film. Each time the funding was set up; it would fall through because someone would die! And when we weren't reeling from the shock of someone's murder, suicide or unusual death; we were weeding through the funding frauds that are rampant within the industry.

And rather than jump into the shallow end of the *Grizzly Adams Trademark Kiddie Pool* that's filled with an endless supply of whiney children; we had decided to write this screenplay in such a way that it wouldn't infringe on the old show. It would however reflect the magic of the real James Capen "Grizzly" Adams in our contemporary "go green" society.

After Chuck's unexpected and sadly tragic death there were a few months when we thought that we could finally heal all the silly problems of the past thirty years. Dan was thrilled by what we all thought would be a *"marriage made in heaven."*

We were flown into Idaho to join the celebration as the local newspaper's announced in Chuck's hometown that finally Dan Haggerty had joined with Grizzly Adams Productions. The plans were laid out and the ideas for the future grew more exciting by the day. We already had verbally committed together to start our *Inside Passage* film first; and then it would soon be followed by another film.

But it wasn't long before a 3rd company slipped into the mix draped in secrecy; and no one realized how much greed, ego and deception they would bring with them. It wasn't long before they had spun their web made of dishonesty and ink - and it was over!

In true Hollywood fashion, the three *"wanna be big shots"* promised the world and delivered only the worthless. It was sad how quickly,

> *...three stooges destroyed
> the marriage that could have been!*

Surprisingly, the disappointment never fazed Dan a bit. I wish I could say that it didn't bother me – but it did. It bothered me because I knew Dan and what he could do. I knew how great it could've been for the original company and everyone else. And... I had truly grown fond of our initial team of people. So when all those dreams were washed away by these three stooges at the last minute – it was frustrating.

In a week or two we went back to work. It was hard at first (for me) to put away the *"what could have beens"* and move on - but I did. It was no problem for Dan at all, he was used to it; after all...

*He's been "doing Hollywood" since he was just a kid.
He never looked back!*

Now There are Two

The more things change
...the more they stay the same.

With "Wild Bill" gone ...it's just the Preacher and the Pirate now. But things are as exciting as ever!

We've just come back from an amazing two week tour in England with some wonderful friends at fabulous venues. One of the events was the national competition for Elvis Tribute Artists The winner of the annual contest moves on to compete for the world title in Memphis during *Elvis Week.* Dan was asked to be one of the celebrity judges because he knew and worked with Elvis.

During his early years as an actor Dan was also an animal trainer, stuntman and a bodybuilder. It was his toned body and six-pack abs that landed him a small role as "Charlie" on the Elvis film *"Girl Happy"* in 1965, starring Elvis and Shelly Fabares.

Dan told the crowd in England that the first time Elvis spoke to him was a comment about his muscular legs. Everyone laughed when Dan said:

"I'll bet I am the only <u>man</u> in the world that can say that Elvis Presley told me that I had nice legs!"

England's Elvis Tribute contest was amazing. Personally, until that event I never realized how incredibly talented the entertainers really are and how hard they work at it. I was amazed at how much England loved Elvis.

On Sunday they held a special Gospel Showcase and all the artists sang the gospel songs that Elvis loved so much. Then they asked me to preach the morning service. I must admit that I have spoken all around the world in churches, on the streets, in stadiums, in Alaskan villages and in fields in the middle of the jungle; but this would be the first time I would preach with *"Elvis"* as my back-up singer!

The old Pirate stays on the move and has appointments somewhere across America every couple of weeks. As for me, the Preacher; I stay busy teaching each week, writing books or traveling to speak somewhere several times a year. I just released my latest book *The Footsteps of the Shepherd* which is listed on Amazon and four new books are on the way.

The Life and Times of Dan Haggerty

In "Tinsel Town" things are still moving along but the cast of characters remains the same. The same old kids are still squabbling about rights and trademarks, and the minutia that comes from their inflated egos.

Dan and I are still on our journey with *Inside Passage,* and the Reality Shows are starting to add Dan's famous beard to the small screen. *American Pickers* recently aired an episode that included showcasing Dan at his home in California. They *"picked"* a painting of Dan riding his Harley, a huge antique door that could have belonged on a pirate ship, and my favorite table that Dan made from a giant tree trunk with the face of an old bearded man carved into its base.

Earlier this year both seasons of the old *Life and Times of Grizzly Adams* television show were released on DVD by CBS. I finally got to watch the show that I never watched in the seventies. It was a lot of fun to see my friend *the pirate,* doing his thing that has brought joy to millions and made Grizzly Adams famous..

As I am writing these words today (on my birthday), I know that next week I will be *back in the booth* with Dan in beautiful Kenab, Utah. The week after that I will begin a preaching trip that will cover eight states and five countries over the next thirty days.

It's exciting that our lives are constantly in fluid motion but we try very hard to never forget what's really important. Sometimes I can't keep up with the Griz and he can't keep up with me.

But when we get home, we both spend our time trying to keep up the grandkids!.

As I close this book I wanted to leave you something from us both that would sum up our views of life.

There are so many ways...
　　....the Preacher, the Pirate, and the Pagan
are different, yet so many ways we're the same!

One of those ways we're the same ... is poetry.
I have loved it all my life and Dan ...wow, he's whole life is full of rhyme and verse. He's constantly reciting poetry with a tone and rhythm that carries you away to a different place and time.

So I asked Dan to give me something personal from him that could say. He called me back with the poem I have often heard him say and recited it from memory. I couldn't think of anything more perfect to describe the pirate:

The Life and Times of Dan Haggerty

"Well my boys, this is what people
think about your old man.

I will try to explain it to you
in my own little way - the best that I can.

They say that I smoke too much;
and that's true – I do.
They say I drink too much too
– and that's true too.

I never like to go to bed; but when do go to bed ...
Oh I never like to have to get up.

I don't pay much attention to time...
And time doesn't pay much attention to me.

I sleep with women
I'm not much on men.

Necrophilia? Oh my God! No my boy...
Just the thought of it ...leaves me cold.

I love poetry - I read it a lot
Just to hear myself breath.

I love nails in my shoes
and a good strong tooth in my jaw
..and a gleam and a twinkle in my eye.

I love hats full of stories
And jokes that I can distribute at will.

But I must say that I'm a wee bit confused at times
For I've lived in a time when men have turned Jews
into soap – that bothers me.

But I've never met a man that I couldn't understand
Or a man that couldn't understand me.

Well I've come to a point, in the time of my life
when I have got something to say.

For you to have the guts to thumb your nose
At the social structures of life
To clip the wings of the human heart
In this cancerous age and time

Oh do I love fireworks in the dull of night
It makes me feel like a boy again

So just take your arms my son and wrapped them
around me - hug me as tight as you can

They may call me Dan ...but don't you ever forget
that I will always be - your old man.

> By: Dan Haggerty

The Life and Times of Dan Haggerty

From me to you ...I only want to say that God has blessed me with a special friend like Dan; and I hope that he can say the same thing about me. Always remember that it only takes one person to change someone's life forever.

The Light of One

One scarce can tell the value
of a kind and giving soul
as along this craggy pilgrim path
we all essay to go.

How many heroes have been lifted
to their place of glory
by nameless hands of love and kindness
that never make the story.

Hidden in the shadowy backdrop
of life's unfolding stage
rare are those unselfish souls
that reckon love for wage.

As stars upon a velvet sky;
or lamps in the dismal night
these flames of warmth and kindness,
are what make our journey bright.

Not one has ever reached
the place of happiness or success

without the aid of one of these
to find strength, comfort and rest.

On this meandering mortal road
nothing can be certain
but one thing we know for sure,
 there is a final curtain.

When all is finished – with nothing left to be said
the dreams for which we spent ourselves
are now fulfilled or dead.

We'll stand before the glorious throne
of the True and Righteous King.
the Judge of all the earth; of whom the angels sing.

And in that moment we'll discover
the treasure and the worth
of those dear souls that gave of themselves
while here upon the earth.

Ponder the moment when His loving hands
are reaching out to thee
saying when you loved your neighbor as yourself –
you did it unto Me.

By: Terry W. Bomar

ABOUT THE AUTHOR
TERRY BOMAR
Minister/Writer/Speaker/Producer

Terry grew up in Memphis, Tenn. and entered the ministry as a very young man. His experience as a speaker, writer, pastor and adventurer has carried him all over the world. He has pastored churches in Tennessee, Hawaii and Florida; and he has been a missionary serving families in third-world countries and a Chaplin working with men and women in County, State and Federal Prisons. He was voted one of the top 25 ministers in America and received an invitation to the U.S. Presidential Inauguration in honor of his work within his local community.

In 1992 he founded Young Adventurers, a children's charity and began working with several celebrity spokespersons which led to his close personal friendship with Dan Haggerty. For more than fifteen years Terry has worked with celebrity management and film production with Dan Haggerty. Since that original meeting Terry has maintained his ministry and charity work, and used his skills to work with dozens of celebrities and production projects. His unique experiences worldwide have given Terry a powerful insight into human nature and made him a fascinating story-teller, motivational speaker and leader. His international experiences have made him a sought after speaker for churches and conferences.

His dedication to people is also demonstrated by his thousands of hours as a youth and family counselor. The combination of his skills with his passion for young people gave birth to his charity 20 years ago. Since then, Young Adventurers has produced many fascinating worldwide travel programs, events and spectacular productions such as their latest *Dream Night* in August of 2012.

52652623R10070

Made in the USA
Charleston, SC
23 February 2016